Warty TOADS

by Meish Goldish

Consultant: Dr. Kenneth L. Krysko
Senior Biological Scientist, Division of Herpetology
Florida Museum of Natural History, University of Florida

BEARPORT
PUBLISHING

New York, New York

Credits
Cover and Title Page, © sylvanworks/iStockphoto, Daniel Rajszczak/Shutterstock, and Maksym Gorpenyuk/Shutterstock; TOC, © Kevin Snair/iStockphoto; 4, © age fotostock/SuperStock; 5, © The Granger Collection, New York; 6L, © David M. Dennis/Animals Animals Enterprises; 6R, © age fotostock/SuperStock; 7, © James P. Rowan; 8T, © Chris Mattison/NHPA/Photoshot; 8B, © Wild Nature Photos/Animals Animals Enterprises; 9, © Piotr Naskrecki/Minden Pictures; 10, © WorldFoto/Alamy; 11T, © Satoshi Kuribayashi/Nature Production/Minden Pictures; 11B, © Kathie Atkinson/Oxford Scientific/Photolibrary; 12T, © Thomas Marent/Visuals Unlimited, Inc.; 12B, © George McCarthy/Nature Picture Library; 13, © Mantis W.F/OSF/Animals Animals Enterprises; 14, © Kenneth L. Krysko; 15T, © Ted Kinsman/Photo Researchers, Inc.; 15B, © Paul Hobson/Nature Picture Library; 16, © Ludwig Werle/Picture Press/Photolibrary; 17, © Dwight Kuhn Photography; 18TL, © Dwight Kuhn Photography; 18TR, © Dwight Kuhn Photography; 18B, © Dwight Kuhn Photography; 19T, © Dwight Kuhn Photography; 19B, © Dwight Kuhn Photography; 20, © Shinji Kusano/Nature Production/Minden Pictures; 21, © Francesco Tomasinelli & Emanuele Biggi/Photo Researchers, Inc.; 22T, © Michael Fogden/Oxford Scientific/Photolibrary; 22B, © Joe McDonald/Visuals Unlimited, Inc; Back Cover, © Kevin Snair/iStockphoto.

Publisher: Kenn Goin
Senior Editor: Lisa Wiseman
Creative Director: Spencer Brinker
Design: Debrah Kaiser
Photo Researcher: Amy Dunleavy

Library of Congress Cataloging-in-Publication Data

Goldish, Meish.
  Warty toads / by Meish Goldish.
     p. cm. — (Amphibiana)
  Includes bibliographical references and index.
  ISBN-13: 978-1-936087-36-5 (library binding)
  ISBN-10: 1-936087-36-7 (library binding)
  1. Toads—Juvenile literature. I. Title.
  QL668.E2G64 2010
  597.8'7—dc22

                              2009031866

For more information, write to Bearport Publishing Company, Inc., 101 Fifth Avenue, Suite 6R, New York, New York 10003. Printed in the United States of America in North Mankato, Minnesota.

112009
090309CGB

10 9 8 7 6 5 4 3 2 1

Contents

Magical Creatures

Do toads have magical powers? About 2,000 years ago, people in ancient Rome thought so. They believed that if they dropped a small bone from the right side of a toad's body into boiling water, it would turn the water cold. They claimed that a bone from the left side of a toad's body could stop angry dogs from attacking anyone who held it.

In ancient times, people believed that toads had the power to make a noisy room quiet.

People also believed there was a jewel called a toadstone inside a toad's head. They thought the jewel, when taken out and placed in a ring or necklace, would heat up or change color when it came near poison. This would alert the person wearing it to danger. Today, people know that these ancient beliefs are false. Nevertheless, toads are still fascinating creatures!

This drawing from 1491 shows a man taking a toadstone from the head of a toad.

In the play *As You Like It*, written about 400 years ago by William Shakespeare, a toad is described as having "a precious jewel in his head."

Toads and Frogs

Many people think that toads look like frogs. That's not too surprising. Toads are actually a type of frog. In fact, both kinds of creatures belong to a group of animals called **amphibians**. These animals usually spend their early life in water and their adult life on land.

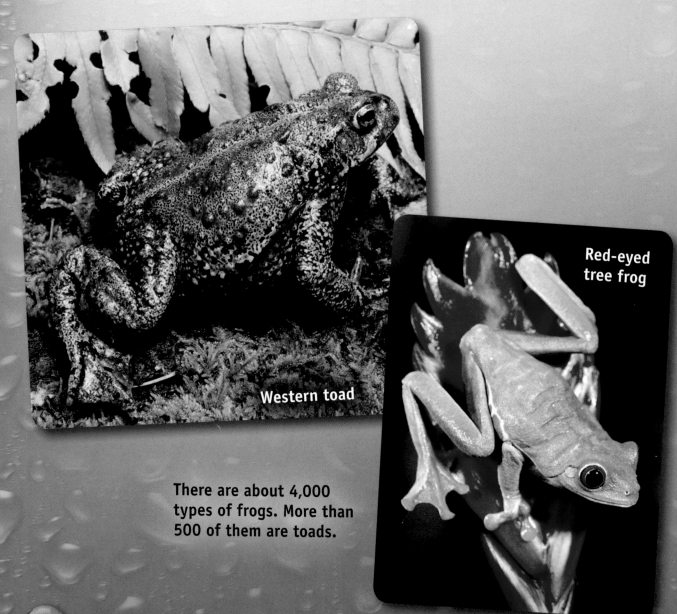

Western toad

Red-eyed tree frog

There are about 4,000 types of frogs. More than 500 of them are toads.

Frogs that are not toads are called **true frogs**. Though closely related, toads and true frogs are different in many ways. True frogs have thin, wet, smooth skin. Toads have thick, dry skin with rough bumps called warts. True frogs have long back legs for leaping high, while toads have short back legs for walking and hopping. Though they have their differences, both true frogs and toads stay mainly on land during their adult lives.

warts

Toads are usually brown, gray, or green.

Many people think that a person can get warts by touching a toad. However, that is not true.

Homes Everywhere

Toads can be found in many places such as forests and parks, mountains and deserts, and lakes and rivers. Some such as spadefoot toads live in **burrows** in the ground. Others such as green climbing toads make their homes in trees.

The spadefoot toad got its name because parts of its back feet are shaped like spades. A spade is a tool that is used for digging. The spadefoot toad uses these parts to dig its way backward into a burrow.

black spade

Toads can be found in both cold and hot places. Those in cold places escape the freezing winter by digging deep into the ground, where it's warmer. They **hibernate** there until the spring. Toads that live in hot places dig down into the ground during the summer to get away from the heat. They might **estivate** in dry mud until the fall brings cooler weather.

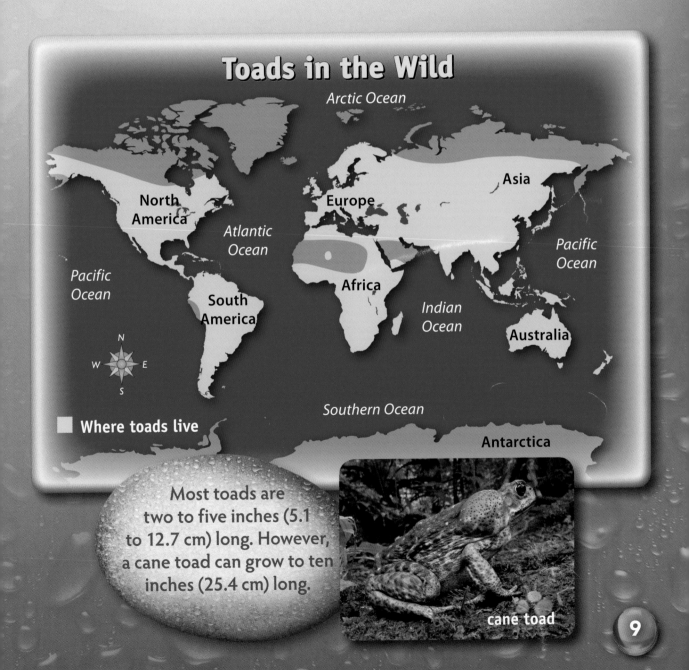

Toads in the Wild

Arctic Ocean

Asia

North America

Europe

Atlantic Ocean

Pacific Ocean

Pacific Ocean

South America

Africa

Indian Ocean

Australia

N
W   E
S

Southern Ocean

■ Where toads live

Antarctica

Most toads are two to five inches (5.1 to 12.7 cm) long. However, a cane toad can grow to ten inches (25.4 cm) long.

cane toad

Out to Eat

Toads hunt other animals for food. They come out at night to find **prey** such as small insects, snails, worms, mice, rats, birds, and snakes.

A toad can see very well, especially at night. While hunting, it can make its **bulging** eyes look in all directions—even behind it. A toad also has great hearing. Its ears, which look like patches of skin behind its eyes, act like drums. Sound bounces off the ears' thinly stretched skin, allowing the toad to feel the **vibrations** of other animals moving nearby.

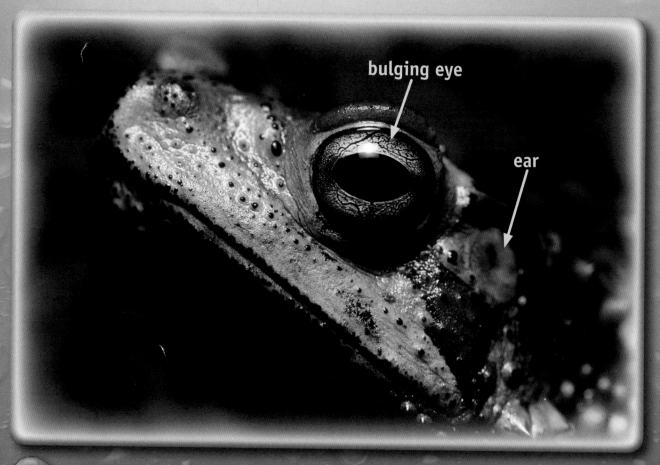

bulging eye

ear

After finding prey, the toad sometimes pretends not to see it to avoid scaring it away. When the victim gets close enough, the toad shoots out its sticky tongue and quickly grabs it.

◁ **The tip of a toad's tongue has a sticky liquid that holds the prey as it is pulled into the toad's mouth.**

Toads have no teeth for chewing their food. Instead, they swallow their meals whole. To help the food go down, toads push their eyes down against the roofs of their mouths. That's why a toad looks like it's blinking while it's eating.

Keeping from Danger

Toads have many ways to keep safe from enemies such as birds and snakes. Some toads have colors that blend in with their surroundings. This **camouflage** makes it hard for other animals to see them. Other toads, such as the common toad, puff up their bodies by gulping air so they look too big for an enemy to swallow.

◁ The crested forest toad is able to camouflage itself among leaves on the forest floor.

This common toad ▷ has puffed itself up in order to defend itself from a snake.

Still other toads have another means of defense—their warts. These bumps produce bad-tasting poison that can harm a **predator**. As a result, animals that eat toads often get sick and can even die. Only a few enemies, such as some skunks, raccoons, and snakes, are not harmed by the poison.

poison

Many animals such as dogs and foxes will spit out a toad after taking just one bite because its poison tastes so awful.

Pairing Off

Most of the year, toads like to be alone. However, they gather together near water when it's time to mate. Mating takes place at different times of the year, depending on the **species** of toad. Each type has its own mating call. For example, male Great Plains toads make loud croaking sounds. Females listen closely to identify males of their species.

△ Many male toads, such as this southern toad, call or sing to females by puffing up their throats like balloons.

Within a few days after mating, females lay two long strands of eggs in the water. Each strand may have thousands of eggs. A sticky jelly covers them. Most species of toads do not stay with their eggs after they are laid.

△ A strand of toad eggs can be more than 70 feet (21.3 m) long. However, many of the eggs are eaten by fish or other animals before they can hatch.

A male midwife toad

After the female lays her eggs, most male and female toads leave them behind. However, some male toads stay around. For example, the male midwife toad protects the eggs by carrying them on his back until they hatch.

Tiny Tadpoles

About a week or so after being laid, a toad's eggs hatch into **tadpoles**. These baby toads have long tails for swimming, but no legs. They look like tiny black fish. The tadpoles, like fish, also have **gills** for breathing. The gills take in **oxygen** from the water.

Tadpoles are also called polliwogs.

A tadpole eats plants and dead insects and even other tadpoles. It is also always in danger of being eaten by animals such as fish, snakes, and giant water beetles. A tadpole is not able to protect itself from enemies the way that an adult toad can.

Tadpoles cannot live outside of water.

△ Tadpoles grow at different rates, depending on the species.

Growth and Change

About three weeks after hatching, a tadpole starts to change into an adult. The change is called **metamorphosis**. First, the tadpole begins to grow legs. Then it slowly loses its gills and starts to develop lungs for breathing. Over the next month, its tail gets shorter and its legs become longer.

Life Cycle of a Toad

① The female toad lays her eggs in water.

② Tadpoles hatch from eggs after about one week.

③ When tadpoles start to lose their gills and tails, their legs and lungs begin to grow.

After being in the water for about ten weeks, the tadpole loses its tail completely. It is now a small toad. It crawls out of the water and starts its life on land—warts and all!

4 With its four legs and shorter tail, the tadpole will soon be ready to live on land.

Toads and frogs are the only amphibians that lose their tails as adults. Salamanders and newts, which are other kinds of amphibians, keep their tails throughout their entire lives.

5 When its lungs are fully developed and its legs are fully grown, the toad moves onto land. It can live for about 25 years.

Helping People

Although people once wrongly believed that toads had magical powers, the animals are actually helpful to people in several ways. For example, farmers like toads because they eat insects that might otherwise harm their crops. A large cane toad can eat 50 crickets in only ten minutes!

△ Some toads can eat as many as 10,000 insects in just one summer.

Spadefoot toads are often used to predict the weather. Before a heavy rain, they come out of the ground and croak. Their call sounds like they are saying, "Rain today! Rain today!" It tells people in the area that a storm is coming.

Toads are helpful in another way, too. Scientists are studying how a toad stretches its tongue to catch prey. They are amazed by the speed and power of the muscles in a toad's mouth. Medical doctors hope that they can use this research to help humans who suffer from muscle disease.

Understanding how a toad uses its muscles may someday be helpful to people.

Toads in Danger

Toads have been on Earth for millions of years. However, scientists fear that some species may now be in danger of dying out completely due to changes in the **environment** and to diseases.

Since toads live both in water and on land, they are threatened by increasing pollution in all parts of their environment. Also, as more ponds and streams are drained to make way for new buildings, more toads lose their homes and there are fewer places for them to breed.

In some places in the world, certain species of toads are already **extinct**. Here are two kinds of toads that are presently in danger.

Golden Toad

- This toad is found only in the mountains of Costa Rica in Central America.
- Thousands of golden toads used to exist. However, not one has been seen in the wild since 1989. Many scientists fear that golden toads are now extinct. Others think that some are still alive but in hiding.
- Scientists think many of the toads may have died as a result of disease, **global warming**, and the destruction of their habitats by builders.

Yosemite Toad

- This toad is found in the Sierra Nevada Mountains in central California.
- In recent years, the Yosemite toad population has dropped by about 50 percent.
- Scientists think many toads have died from chemical pollution of the water, cattle and cars crushing the toads on roads, and deadly diseases.

Glossary

amphibians (am-FIB-ee-uhnz) animals that usually spend part of their lives in water and part on land

bulging (BUHL-jing) sticking out like a lump

burrows (BUR-ohz) tunnels or holes in the ground made by animals

camouflage (KAM-uh-flahzh) coloring that makes animals look like their surroundings

environment (en-VYE-ruhn-muhnt) the area where an animal or plant lives, and all the things, such as weather, that affect that place

estivate (ESS-tuh-vate) to spend the summer in a deep sleep to escape the heat

extinct (ek-STINGKT) when a kind of plant or animal has died out

gills (GILZ) the body parts of a water animal that are used for breathing

global warming (GLOH-buhl WORM-ing) a slow, steady rise in the air temperature around the world, caused by gases that collect in the air and prevent the sun's heat from escaping

hibernate (HYE-bur-nate) to spend the winter in a deep sleep to escape the cold

metamorphosis (*met*-uh-MOR-fuh-siss) a series of changes that some kinds of animals go through as they develop from eggs to adults

midwife (MID-wife) a person or animal who helps a female in childbirth

oxygen (OK-suh-juhn) a colorless gas found in the air or water

predator (PRED-uh-tur) an animal that hunts other animals for food

prey (PRAY) animals that are hunted by other animals for food

species (SPEE-sheez) groups that animals are divided into, according to similar characteristics

tadpoles (TAD-pohlz) young toads or frogs before they become adults

true frogs (TROO FRAWGS) all types of frogs except for toads

vibrations (vye-BRAY-shunz) rapid back-and-forth movements that can be felt

Index

Bibliography

Clarke, Barry. *Amazing Frogs and Toads.* New York: Knopf (1990).

Maruska, Edward. *Amphibians: Creatures of the Land and Water.* New York: Franklin Watts (1994).

Miller, Sara Swan. *Frogs and Toads: The Leggy Leapers.* New York: Franklin Watts (2000).

Read More

Harman, Amanda. *Toads.* Danbury, CT: Grolier (2001).

Jacobs, Lee. *Toads.* San Diego, CA: Blackbirch Press (2002).

Murray, Julie. *Toads.* Edina, MN: ABDO Publishing (2003).

Learn More Online

To learn more about toads, visit
www.bearportpublishing.com/Amphibiana

About the Author

Meish Goldish has written more than 200 books for children. He lives in Brooklyn, New York.